Life in the Desert

Life in the
Desert

Ron Fridell

Watts LIBRARY™

Franklin Watts
A Division of Scholastic Inc.
New York • Toronto • London • Auckland • Sydney
Mexico City • New Delhi • Hong Kong
Danbury, Connecticut

Note to readers: Definitions for words in **bold** can be found in the Glossary at the back of this book.

Photographs © 2005: Corbis Images: 5 bottom, 21 (Yann Arthus-Bertrand), 22, 23 (Anthony Bannister/ Gallo Images), 18 top (Steve Bein), 47 (Dean Conger), 40 (John Conrad), cover (Jose Fuste Raga), 18 bottom (Elisa Haberer), 25 (Jeremy Horner), 33 (Dewitt Jones), 26 (Ludovic Maisant), 31 (Joe McDonald), 6 (Phil Schermeister), 17 bottom (Scott T. Smith), 44 (Vanni Archive); Getty Images/ Carsten Peter: 9; Minden Pictures: 42 (Michael & Patricia Fogden), 19 (Tui De Roy); National Geographic Image Collection: 2 (D. Brown/Panstock/Panoramic Images), 34 (Bill Curtsinger), 12, 13 (Warren Marr/Panoramic Images), 17 top (Joel Sartore); Nature Picture Library Ltd.: 29 (Jeff Foott), 39 (David Shale); Peter Arnold Inc./Martin Harvey: 11; Photo Researchers, NY: 16 (Canadian Space Agency/RADARSAT/ NASA), 30 (Gregory G. Dimijian, M.D.), 5 top, 37 (T. D. W. Friedmann), 49 (Lowell Georgia), 38 (Craig K. Lorenz), 10 (Tom McHugh).

Illustrations by: Bob Italia

The photograph on the cover shows the Sahara Desert. The photograph opposite the title page shows a rugged road in the Sonoran Desert in Arizona.

Library of Congress Cataloging-in-Publication Data

Fridell, Ron.
 Life in the desert / Ron Fridell.
  p. cm. — (Watts library)
 Includes bibliographical references and index.
 ISBN 0-531-12384-7
1. Desert ecology—Juvenile literature. I. Title. II. Series.

 QH541.5.D4F75 2005
 577.54—dc22   2004027254

Contents

This desert landscape in Death Valley, California, is called the Devil's Golf Course. When an ancient lake evaporated, it left behind tons of salt, which formed these rocklike lumps.

Chapter One

The Extreme Biome

When you imagine a **desert,** what do you picture? Close your eyes and imagine.

Did you picture endless seas of sand? Lots of people picture nothing but dry and lifeless sand **dunes.** Well, they're right about one thing—deserts are the driest **biome** on Earth. A biome is a region with its own life forms and climates. A desert is a region in which less than 10 inches (25 centimeters) of rain falls per year. Compare that with the

80 inches (203 cm) that fall on **rain forests,** the wettest biome on Earth.

All deserts are dry. But low rainfall is the only characteristic they share. Each desert is unique. Deserts tend to be places of extremes. Some are seas of sand, while others are nothing but rock. Some lie hundreds of feet below sea level, while others are perched thousands of feet above Earth's surface. Some deserts sizzle. They're right up there among the hottest spots on Earth. Others are so frigid that a year-round ice sheet thousands of feet thick covers every square inch of land.

Hidden Life

What about life in these extreme desert landscapes? In parts of the Sahara in northern Africa, you could walk hundreds of miles and never see another living thing. But all deserts have at least some life, and many deserts are teeming with it.

Deserts don't always look lively, though. Have you ever watered a wilting plant? Then you've seen how it can perk right up. A rare rainstorm can work the same sort of magic on a lifeless-looking desert. In a matter of days, seeds sprout, and flowers spring up. Eggs hatch, and streams and pools come alive with aquatic animals.

Fish in the desert? Yes. Shrimps and toads, too, and mammals and reptiles and insects and birds. All sorts of animals, from fleas to scorpions to bobcats to eagles, inhabit

Traveling through the Sahara by camel, you may not see another living thing for days on end.

Pollution and loss of habitat because of human activities have made the desert pupfish an endangered species.

Salty Fish

Desert waters can be three times as salty as the ocean. Desert pupfish have adapted to this extremely salty water. Thousands of these tiny creatures thrive in warm desert pools and springs where other fish could last a few days at most.

the desert. Thousands of species of plants live there as well, from inch-high dwarf cacti to towering palms.

Desert biomes rank near the top in biodiversity, the number of different life forms that inhabit a region. Only rain forests are home to more different kinds of plant and animal species. This diverse desert life includes 800 million *Homo sapiens*. That's right—13 percent of the world's human population live in deserts.

Deserts cover about one-fifth of Earth's total land surface. In this book, you'll learn what makes each desert unique. You'll also discover the surprising strategies that plants, animals, and people use to survive and thrive in one of the most extreme biomes on Earth.

A sand-burrowing scorpion with its poisonous stinger tail

The heat-cracked floor of the Mojave, a hot California desert, looks like it could not sustain life, but it does.

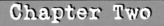

Chapter Two

Hot and Cold Recipes

How are deserts created? Let's start with hot deserts. The world's all-time hottest temperature was recorded in the Sahara: 136.4 degrees Fahrenheit (58 degrees Celsius). The hottest temperature in the United States was recorded in another desert location—Death Valley, California: 134° F (57° C).

Why is the air in the desert so dry? The key factors that create dry air are sunlight, oceans, rain forests, and air currents. Here's how they all work

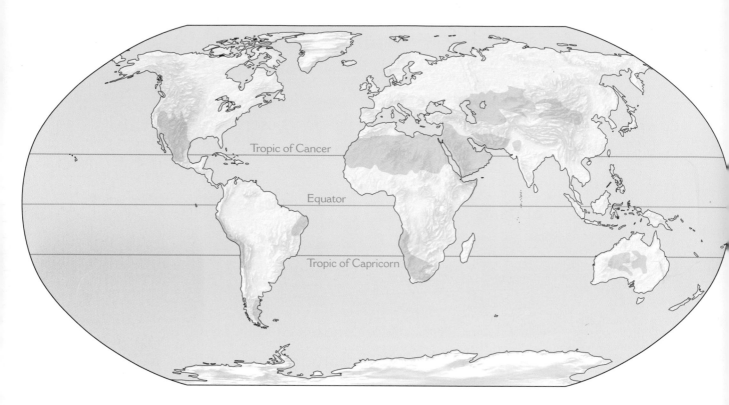

Tropic of Cancer

Equator

Tropic of Capricorn

Which parts of the world have the most deserts?

together to make a hot desert. Temperatures are hottest near the equator, where sunlight is strongest. It's strongest there because the sun is more directly overhead at the equator than anywhere else on Earth. When you rotate a globe 360 degrees, you see that oceans and rain forests straddle the equator all around the world. Lots of water **evaporates** from these oceans and rain forests in the form of invisible water vapor— and hot air can hold lots of moisture. As this invisible gas rises, it cools and condenses into visible droplets. Then clouds form, and soon the droplets fall back down on the rain forests as rain, leaving the air above dry.

This high and dry equatorial air now begins a very long journey. Some of it heads toward the North Pole, the rest toward the South Pole. For a few thousand miles these air currents stay hot and dry—a perfect climate for a hot desert. That's why most of the world's hot deserts lie between the Tropics of Cancer and Capricorn.

Climograph of Death Valley

	120° F 49° C						115°	113°				
					109°				105°			
	100° F 38° C	**Average High Temperature**		99°						92°		
			89°				86°	84°				
	80° F 27° C	80°			80°				75°		76°	
	73°			71°								65°
	66°		62°						61°			
	60° F 16° C	54°									47°	
	46°											
	40° F 4° C											
	39°										37°	

Average Low Temperature

Jan	Feb	Mar	Apr	May	Jun	Jul	Aug	Sep	Oct	Nov	Dec

Average Precipitation in Inches

| 0.29 in 0.74 cm | 0.50 in 1.27 cm | 0.33 in 0.83 cm | 0.13 in 0.33 cm | 0.07 in 0.18 cm | 0.05 in 0.13 cm | 0.13 in 0.33 cm | 0.14 in 0.36 cm | 0.18 in 0.46 cm | 0.09 in 0.23 cm | 0.19 in 0.48 cm | 0.16 in 0.41 cm |

A climograph is created by scientists to show a location's precipitation and average temperatures during the year. This climograph gives information about Death Valley in California.

Cold Deserts

How cold can cold deserts get? Extremely cold. Vostok, Antarctica, holds the world's record for the all-time lowest temperature: −128.6° F (−89.2° C). Cold deserts come in three types: coastal, rain shadow, and high altitude.

The Atacama is a cold **coastal desert.** It lies alongside the cold Pacific Ocean in the South American nation of Chile. Cold air can't hold much moisture. The cold ocean current flowing northward from Antarctica keeps the air above the Atacama Desert so cool and dry that rain hardly ever falls. In some places in the Atacama, not a drop of rain has fallen in more than four hundred years! The cold Atacama is Earth's driest desert.

The Great Basin Desert is a cold **rain shadow desert.** Every mountain range has a wet side, where most of the rain falls, and a dry side. The dry side lies in the "rain shadow," the

Moving Heat

Ocean currents move 30 percent of the sun's heat energy around the planet. Air currents circulate the rest.

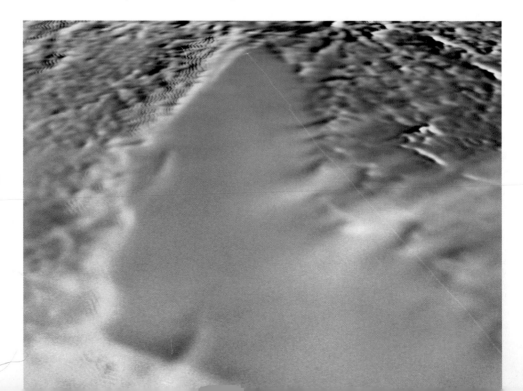

Beneath the area of smooth ice lie the waters of Lake Vostok. This satellite photo shows the coldest spot on Earth, in the high-altitude desert of Antarctica.

area that gets hardly any rain. The Great Basin Desert is actually a series of deserts that lie on the dry side—the eastern slopes—of the Sierra and Cascade mountains in the western United States. When the moist air from the Pacific Ocean meets the western slopes of these mountains, it rises and cools. By the time this air makes its

A delivery truck winds its way through Chile's extremely cold and dry Atacama Desert.

way up over the mountains, the moisture has fallen in the form of rain or snow. Then, as this dry air flows down the eastern slopes, it heats up—a perfect climate to make a desert in the rain shadow, on the eastern side. The Gobi Desert in central Asia is another rain shadow desert.

The thin cirrus clouds that float above Utah's Great Salt Lake hold no moisture for this rain shadow desert.

Nearly all the moisture falls on the far side of the distant mountains. That's why this land is part of Mongolia's Gobi Desert.

A traveler meets people who live "on top of the world," in Tibet's Chang Tang, Earth's highest desert.

High-altitude deserts are cold because the higher above Earth's surface you are, the colder the air is. The world's highest desert, the Chang Tang in northern Tibet, sits on a plateau that rises to an altitude of 19,000 feet (5,791 meters) above sea level. That's nearly 4 miles (6.4 kilometers) high! Latitude also plays a part in making deserts cold.

Latitude is the distance north or south of the equator, measured in degrees. The Great White Desert of Antarctica lies far south of the equator, where the sunlight hits Earth at such a shallow angle that very little heat energy ever reaches the ground. Also, Antarctica rests on a rock surface 8,000 feet (2,440 m) above sea level. Together, this far-south latitude and high altitude are perfect conditions for a cold desert.

Tourists who want a real adventure visit the frozen deserts of Antarctica.

19

Rain, Fog, Dew

Water is the most precious ingredient in any desert, hot or cold. Water is required for life to exist. Deserts get some of their life-giving moisture from rain. Rain in the desert is welcome, unless it falls in raging storms. In other biomes, thick soils absorb most rainfall before it can run downhill or overflow riverbanks. But desert soils are thin. They can't soak up much water, so stream beds and riverbeds fill up quickly and overflow.

If enough rain falls, flash floods can erupt. Torrents of crashing water hurl stones and boulders down mountainsides and along streams. Flash floods can erupt so suddenly that people living or camping nearby may get trapped. In 1976 in Denver, Colorado, for example, a wall of water 19 feet (5.8 m) high swept along a river where people were camping, and 140 people died. More people drown in deserts each year

Some deserts are like planets. This one in the Canadian Arctic is a lot like the planet Mars, where deserts are much colder and drier than here on Earth.

The Eye Finds the River

From atop a desert hill, you can easily trace the line of a dry riverbed with your eyes. Just follow the lines of green plants on both sides. They grow there even when the riverbed is dry.

than die of thirst. Fortunately, flash floods are rare.

During normal desert rain-storms, riverbeds suddenly fill with swiftly moving water, and dry lake beds fill up. Afterwards, plants quickly bloom and blossom. The results can be awesome, drawing tourists from around the world hoping to see colorful shows of desert life. The most spectacular sights are in the Namib Desert along the western coast of Namibia in southern Africa. Each year in October, desert rains bring millions of flowers to life. For a few weeks, for hundreds of miles in all directions, vast fields of desert flowers are all you see.

Rain is not the only source of desert moisture. Fog forms in cold coastal deserts such as the Namib. Cold ocean currents keep evaporation low and rain to a minimum, but wet ocean air sometimes blows inland and condenses into fog.

Dew is another source of precious desert moisture. Israel's Negev Desert has about two hundred "dew days"

A desert in full bloom? For a precious few weeks each year, this part of the Namib in southern Africa looks just like a meadow in spring.

each year. Water vapor condenses on night-cooled surfaces, and plants and animals use clever strategies to collect it during the night and early morning.

Oases and Rivers

All hot deserts and most cold deserts have a few pockets of moist, green land called **oases.** When we imagine an oasis, we usually picture a few palm trees and a circle of grass around a tiny pool. Some oases are small—about 2.5 acres (1 hectare) in area. But many oases are larger, and a few are vast. The Al-Hasa Oasis in the Arabian Desert covers 30,000 acres (12,140 ha). How vast is that? Picture an average suburban house and yard, which take up about 0.25 acre (0.1 ha). Now multiply that picture by 120,000.

Where do oases get their water? Some get it from **aquifers,** made up of porous rocks that store water underground like a sponge. Often this is **fossil water,** accumulated millions of years ago when the climate was wet and when lakes, forests, and marshes covered the land. A natural obstruction below ground, usually a wall of clay or crushed rock, forms a horizontal dam, which pushes this stored water to the surface.

Other oases get their water from rivers. Oases in Chile's Atacama Desert are fed by rivers flowing down from high in the Andes Mountains. The valley running along Earth's longest river, the Nile, which flows for 4,160 miles (6,694 km), is mostly one long oasis. Farmers in Egypt use the Nile's life-giving waters to grow crops in the Sahara Desert.

Oases are the most concentrated pockets of life in any desert. Each oasis is its own mini-world of plants and

animals. There is life in other parts of a desert, too, where a surprising number of living things have managed to adapt to this harsh biome, each in its own way.

Even the super-dry Atacama Desert has plant life. The wide spaces between the plants show how limited the water supply is.

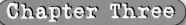

Chapter Three

Adaptable Plants

When you look down on a rain forest from above, you see a leafy green sea of plants crowded together and hardly any open space. When you look down on many deserts, you see green plants dotting the land, with lots of bare space in between. To survive, desert plants must put space between themselves.

Green plants get energy through **photosynthesis,** a process that requires carbon dioxide, sunlight, the chlorophyll in plant tissues, and the most crucial ingredient of all, water. Desert plants cannot survive without adapting to the fact that water is scarce. Most desert plants are small, widely spaced shrubs. The drier the soil, the wider apart these plants space themselves. That way the plants in a desert landscape can share the scarce supply of water.

Storing Water

A rainstorm in a desert is a rare event. Some desert plants must go without fresh water for a year at a time. They wouldn't survive these periods of drought if they couldn't collect and store water when it is available.

Storage begins at the roots, where water enters a plant. Some desert shrubs have shallow root systems that branch out far and wide to soak up moisture from a great area. The extra water gets stored in the core of the roots. Then, during a drought, the plant turns to this stored water for photosynthesis. The creosote bush is a desert plant that stores water in its shallow root system.

Other desert plants have a **taproot.** This is one long root that grows straight down and anchors the plant. Some tap-roots are as long as 80 feet (24 m). Tap roots search for the water table. That's the level below the ground where the soil is soaked with water. The prickly desert plant known as hawthoria has a taproot.

Hawthorias also have a unique feature among plants: a clear window. Hawthorias grow almost entirely underground to find shelter from the hot desert sunlight. Only the tips of the leaves peek out above the surface. But without sunlight, hawthorias could not photosynthesize. That's why, at the tip of each leaf, you'll find a clear window that lets in sunlight. With its deep taproot and leaf-tip window, the hawthoria has adapted to hot-desert living.

King Cactus

The cardon cactus is the biggest cactus on Earth. Some grow to be 70 feet (21 m) tall and to weigh 25 tons (22.7 metric tons). Cardons grow in the San Felipe Desert of the Baja California Peninsula. In winter, their long arms sprout dozens of trumpet-shaped white flowers.

This thick and tall cardon cactus grows on a desert island in Baja California's Sea of Cortez.

After a rain shower, flowers sometimes sprout on the creosote plant. When you rub the waxy little leaves together and hold them to your nose, they smell sharp and smoky.

The cactus is another hot-desert survivor. Its secret lies in its stem, which is 90 percent water. Cactus stems are pleated. They expand like an accordion to store water when it rains. Then, during a drought when the plant must use its store of water to survive, the pleats contract.

Most desert plants have tiny leaves. The reason is **transpiration,** the transfer of water from the leaves and stems of plants to the atmosphere in the form of water vapor. This process allows green plants to take in the carbon dioxide they must have for photosynthesis. They take it in through **stomata,** little holes in their leaves and stems. But for every molecule of carbon dioxide that plants take in, they lose many molecules of water. So the tinier their leaves, the less water plants lose to transpiration.

Some desert plants have no leaves at all. They have sharp thorns or spines instead. The prickly spines on a cactus stem help bring in moisture. The spines collect water from desert dew, then direct it downward from spine to spine to the soil, where the shallow roots take it in. As an extra bonus, cactus spines give the stem a little shade.

Sharp and Deadly Defenses

Desert plants must develop strategies to avoid predators, animals that eat plants and other animals. Some plants use their leaves and spines to ward off **herbivores,** or plant eaters. The creosote bush has leaves that smell and taste bad to insects and wildlife. Stinging nettles give a needlelike sting from the hairs on their leaves and stems. Cacti rely on their painfully sharp spines to keep predators at a distance. One cactus species, the jumping cholla, has long spines that detach and stick to anything that so much as touches them. Ask anyone who's had an encounter with a jumping cholla. They'll tell you that these barbed spines are hard to remove and can cause painful wounds.

Some desert plants and animals develop **symbiotic relationships.** They cooperate to keep one another alive and

Those Lovable Pricklies

Some prickly cacti have sweet, lovable names because of what they happen to look like. With its brown and tan spines, the teddy bear cholla looks from a distance a bit like that cuddly toy. The old man cactus is named for its spines, which look like long white hair.

Ants inhabit these black growths, called galls, on desert acacia trees. At a moment's notice, the ants will stream out to attack invading herbivores.

well. Bullhorn acacia trees and ants have an interesting symbiotic relationship. The key is the acacia's sharp thorns, which are 1 inch (2.5 cm) long. A colony of ants lives at the swollen base of each thorn. The ants drill into the thorn and hollow it out. If a beetle or some other plant eater tries to take a bite of the acacia, the ants immediately launch a savage attack to drive off the invader. In return, the acacia provides the ants with sugary liquid nectar it produces at the base of its leaf stalks. This high-energy food supply gives the ants the nourishment they need to survive.

Sleeping Beauties

Some desert plants survive by taking long naps. These plants stay **dormant** for most of the year. Dormancy is like sleep. During this slumber, their lives are on hold. Then, when at last the rains come, they awaken in a flash, like Sleeping Beauty in the fairy tale when the handsome prince gives her a kiss.

The ocotillo, or fire thorn branch, is a hot desert Sleeping Beauty. During droughts, it sheds its leaves and retreats into dormancy. When rain falls, the ocotillo perks right up and grows its leaves back in a matter of days.

Cold deserts have their Sleeping Beauties as well. One is lichen. These tiny plants grow during summers in the **polar deserts** of the Arctic and Antarctic. Lichens usually grow on rocks and look something like moss. They are not a single organism but a dense, compact community of algae and fungi that all live as one. The air must be above freezing for the lichens to photosynthesize. When the temperature falls too low, they become dormant until the air warms up enough for them to spring to life again.

Life in Fast Forward

Some desert plants live for only a single season. Many of these plants are wildflowers, such as daisies and asters. These plants must find a way to sprout quickly from their seeds, grow, mature, and scatter new seeds on the desert floor, all in the brief time the desert comes alive with rainfall. Otherwise, these species will not survive.

How do the seeds know when to start this hurry-up process? A certain combination of heat, moisture, and sunlight sets things in motion—and the race begins. The plants must send up stalks, bloom, and make and scatter seeds, all before the rainwater evaporates and the heat dries the plants up.

One plant from the Sahara scatters its seeds only after its life has ended. The rose of Jericho sheds its leaves during its last few hours of life. Then its bare stem and branches dry up and fold inward into a lightweight ball that the desert winds easily pick up. As it rolls along, the rose of Jericho sheds its seeds for the winds to pick up and scatter. A plant just like it grows in the American Southwest—the tumbleweed. The newly scattered seeds stay dormant until the next desert rainfall, then quickly sprout and bring the next generation of plants to life.

Locked-Up Water

In a polar desert the rare bits of moisture that fall are added to the icy surface. This frozen moisture has been accumulating over billions of years. An estimated 70 percent of all Earth's fresh water is locked up in ice sheets and glaciers.

As the wind rolls them along, tumbleweeds scatter their seeds at random.

This turkey vulture views desert life from its spiny perch.

Chapter Four

Ingenious Animals

During the daytime in hot deserts, most desert animals stay below ground or beneath rocks to keep cool. Imagine you could stand in a desert in daylight and watch all the animals appear for one magical moment. Make it the Sonoran Desert in southeastern Arizona. What would you see?

All around you are tens of thousands of species of birds, mammals, reptiles, amphibians, and insects. Looking up, you see hundreds of different birds, ranging from the huge turkey vulture to the teeny elf owl. Looking down, you see lizards and rattlesnakes and toads. Looking closer, you see mice and spiders and hundreds of ants. If you had super-magnified vision, you could also see all the ticks, fleas, and mites.

The Sonoran Desert is rich in animal species, but nearly all deserts are home to all sorts of animals. In one important way these animals are like desert plants. Each species survives by adapting to the desert in its own way.

Hard Traveling

Animals must be mobile to survive, and deserts can make moving from place to place hard work. Sandstorms are one reason travel is difficult. That's why camels, also known as the "ships of the desert," have two sets of eyelids. The first set is transparent and protects against the driving sand while allowing the camel to keep moving on, even in furious sandstorms. Throughout history, camels were the chief means of transportation in many deserts.

Sand makes for hard traveling in another way. If you've ever walked on sand, you know it gives way easily and makes your feet slide and sink in, especially on loosely packed sand dunes. That's why fringe-toed lizards have long, pointed scales on their toes. These scales give the lizards extra traction, like extra-thick treads on car tires.

Jackrabbits have their own way of coping with the

Booming Dunes

Startled desert travelers have reported hearing mysterious sounds in the distance. Some describe these sounds as booming. Other travelers describe them as singing, moaning, or roaring noises. The source of these sounds is mini-landslides on tall sand dunes. Millions of rolling, vibrating grains make the ghostly sounds while sliding down the dunes' steep slopes.

Long legs put some cooling distance between the camel's body and hot desert sands.

The hairless insides of its long ears release body heat to help cool off this desert jackrabbit.

slippery sand. They jump when they travel. Jumping also keeps them off the hot desert surface.

Some desert animals travel by "swimming" through sand. The sandfish of northern Africa—not really a fish but a lizard—has a streamlined body that ends in a pointed tail. This sleek shape helps it journey across seas of sand by moving from side to side in a swimming motion. Sandfish often travel just

beneath the surface. A sandfish may "swim" 3 miles (5 km) in a single night.

The sandfish's streamlined body slides smoothly across— and beneath—the desert sands.

Finding Food

Plants make their own food, but animals must find theirs. Some desert animals are **carnivores,** or meat eaters, with ingenious strategies for catching their prey.

One ingenious carnivore is the tiny insect known as the ant lion. It's favorite prey is ants. To trap them, it digs a cone-shaped pit and waits at the bottom, peeking up from beneath the sand. When it spies a passing ant, it tosses sand upward. This triggers a landslide that sends the ant tumbling straight into the ant lion's powerful jaws. Then this fierce insect sucks its prey dry.

The sandfish lies in wait beneath the surface, too. When it feels vibrations from a creature above, it "swims" up quickly to grab its prey. The sidewinding adder snake also buries itself, leaving only its eyes above the surface. When lizards or other small animals come near, it kills them with a quick bite from its poisonous fangs.

The red spitting cobra of eastern Africa is another snake that uses poisonous venom to slay its prey. The cobra can spit its venom as far as 6.5 feet (2 m). It consumes lizards, birds, and small mammals, but it will attack humans if cornered. People have gone blind when hit in the eye with venom from a red spitting cobra.

This red spitting cobra's flared hood shows that it's primed for attack.

Storing Food

Some desert animals can go days and even months without eating anything at all. So when they find food, they store away as much as they can. Each species has its own way of storing food. Camels store fat in their humps, and some desert lizards store fat in their tails. Mongolian gerbils use their chubby cheeks as containers, which they fill with seeds. Back in their burrows, they unload their cheeks.

The prize for the most unusual way of storing food goes to the honeypot ant, found in deserts all over the world. Picture an ant hanging helplessly upside down from the roof of its underground nest. Then picture other ants feeding it nectar gathered from desert plants. This plant nectar is found in large quantities only after a rare desert rain. So the worker ants quickly bring it back and regurgitate it into the throats of the hanging ants. Soon, the hanging ants look like golden balloons, with abdomens swollen to ten times their normal size. For the rest of their lives, the honeypot ants hang there, all bloated and golden. During droughts, other ants feed off their stored nectar.

Escaping Heat

Desert heat can kill, especially during dry times of the year. That's why hot-desert animals must find ways to keep their body temperatures cool. Different desert animals have different ways of cooling off. Birds have the best strategy of all. All they need to do is fly high where the air is cooler. Other hot-desert animals are not so lucky. Many remain in their dens or burrows during the day, where temperatures are a little cooler. These burrowing animals include bats, snakes, rodents, foxes, and skunks.

The animals that do venture outside during the day must find shade, and shade in the desert is hard to find. As the sun moves across the sky, ants circle around twigs to stay on the shady side. Ant lions lying in wait for prey maneuver around

Sweet Insect Treats

Aborigines, the native peoples of Australia, use some desert insects as food and medicine. A favorite treat is the honeypot ant. They bite into its bloated hind end and savor the nectar.

their pits to keep in the shade. African ground squirrels make their own shade by holding up their fluffy tails like umbrellas while they hunt for nuts and seeds.

Some hot-desert animals use the same strategy as plants use to avoid the heat. During especially hot times of the year, they become dormant. The eggs of brine shrimp can remain dormant in dry lake beds for years if they have to. Like the seeds of desert plants, the eggs are tough enough to resist years of drought. When rain finally does come, the eggs hatch within forty-eight hours. The shrimp quickly become adults that lay eggs before the lake bed dries up.

When is a furry tail like an umbrella? When it belongs to an African ground squirrel.

Getting Water

Desert animals have all sorts of strategies for getting water. Some dig down for it. Large mammals, such as bobcats and badgers, dig holes in dry riverbeds until they reach the water table. Some desert insects suck or lick up the dew and fog that condenses on plants. Others take in plant fluids, such as nectar from flowers and sap from stems.

Some seed-eating birds, such as the sand grouse of Asia, fly their water in. During nesting season, the adult birds wing their way to nearby water holes, walk into the water, and soak it up with their belly feathers. Then they fly back to the nest, where the babies peck at the parents' soaked feathers to take in precious moisture.

But no desert animal has a more ingenious strategy for getting water than the darkling beetle. Imagine this: It is dawn in the Namib Desert in southwestern Africa, where waves of sand meet waves of cold ocean water. A small black beetle faces the ocean, perched on the crest of a dune. A cool breeze pushes thick fog off the cold water into the night-cooled desert. The beetle faces directly into this breeze with its head down, bottom up, and wings spread wide. Shiny knobs and channels cover its waxy shell. As the fog rolls up the dune, droplets condense on the knobs, slide into the channels, and flow downward, straight to the beetle's open mouth. The darkling beetle, standing on its head, drinks the ocean fog.

Beetle Brainstorm

Inventors have designed tents that capture moisture from desert fog and dew. The idea for their design came from watching the darkling beetle at work.

43

Hollowed-out rock homes below the hot desert surface keep Matmata's inhabitants cool.

Chapter Five

Inventive People

The desert is not an easy place to live. Desert dwellers must be determined and inventive. Let's look at how different people have adapted to desert extremes. We'll start with traditional desert people who still live very much like their ancestors did.

There is a town in the Sahara Desert where people live underground. It is Matmata, in the north African country of Tunisia. By day, the heat can be overpowering, while temperatures at night can be bone-chilling.

To escape these desert extremes, Matmata's one thousand inhabitants have dug and chipped out cave homes 30 feet (9 m) below the surface. At the bottom of craterlike pits, they dig rooms into the pit walls and then start tunneling upward. As a family grows, more rooms are added inward and upward. Family members use rope ladders or rocky toeholds to climb from room to room.

Temperatures below ground are steadier and less extreme than temperatures at the surface. The cave homes of the Matmatans are their way of adapting to the desert's harsh climate. The cave-dwellers of Matmata have lived in their cave homes for more than two thousand years.

Traditional People

The Matmatans chose to settle in one spot. Other desert dwellers known as **nomads** move from place to place, taking everything they own with them. This includes their livestock—sheep, goats, horses, and cattle. Because desert vegetation is thin and sparse, nomads graze their herds for only a few weeks in one spot before moving on to another. Nomads move ten times a year on average. By the time they return to an area, the vegetation has had time to grow back for grazing.

Mongolian nomads in central Asia live in round, tentlike structures called yurts. The walls are sheets of felt made of sheep's wool laid over a skeleton of wooden ribs that curve in at the top like a crown.

The Bedouin nomads of the Arabian Desert make their tents out of cloth woven of hair from the goats they raise. In a rainstorm, this goat-hair cloth soaks up water and expands to make the tent waterproof. The walls are loose and airy, with wide openings to let in the wind.

Traditional desert people have adapted their clothing for desert extremes. The Bedouins, who live in hot deserts, wear thin, flowing robes. The nomadic herdsmen of Tibet, who live in cold deserts, wear thick robes with long sleeves and high collars. The robes are made of sheepskin, as are their warm hats.

The nomads' animals give them material to make clothing and shelter. These animals also provide nomads with food. Traditional desert people eat sheep, goats, camels, and chickens, as well as the milk and eggs these animals supply. Fruits and vegetables are harder to come by. Deserts are

So How Do They Do It?

Some desert people have a seemingly uncanny ability to find their way through desert landscapes of shifting sands and bare rock along invisible routes from one watering hole to another. How can they do this without having landmarks to guide them? Like sailors at sea, they find their way by using the stars to guide them.

This Mongolian man's yurt gives him a solid, lightweight dwelling he can take with him wherever he goes.

Along the Silk Road

In the past, caravans with hundreds of camels carried travelers and supplies across vast stretches of desert, stopping at oases along the way. The most famous caravan routes of all made up what was known as the Silk Road, a series of routes linking China to Europe. Caravans brought silk, spices, and other exotic goods along the Silk Road across the Gobi Desert in northern China and southern Mongolia. Eventually this merchandise found its way to eager buyers in Europe. The traders moving between lands in caravans also spread new ideas, customs, and religions, linking faraway civilizations to one another. The thirteenth- and fourteenth-century explorer Marco Polo wrote about his travels along the Silk Road in The Travels of Marco Polo.

short of the thick soil and abundant water that most crops need to grow. That's why most traditional desert people, other than nomads, live in or near oases. These lush islands of comfort in the harsh desert offer more than just water. They have rich, fertile soil where farmers grow dates, olives, peaches, rice, corn, and other crops.

Modern Life, Modern Problems

More people live in deserts today than ever before, but most of them live in modern cities. The North American cities of Las Vegas, Nevada; Los Angeles, California; Phoenix, Arizona; and Salt Lake City, Utah are all built on land that used to be wild desert. So are Tel Aviv, Israel, and Riyadh, Saudi Arabia, in the Middle East.

These and other modern desert cities exist because people adapt the desert to their needs. They use air-condition-

ing to manufacture cool indoor climates. They transform barren desert land into lush farmland by pulling vast amounts of water from deep within Earth. Saudi Arabia is one of the driest nations on the planet, yet vast fields of cotton and wheat grow in the Saudi desert. This is possible because of irrigation, the process of moving water from one place to another to water crops.

People have found oil, gold, and diamonds in deserts, but water is still the most precious desert resource. Much of the water that supplies modern desert cities and irrigates crops comes from aquifers of fossil water that accumulated thousands of years ago. Fossil water can never be replaced. Someday these aquifers may all be used up. Then oases will start shrinking, and desert rivers will begin drying up.

This pipe releases moisture little by little to irrigate dry desert land without wasting precious water.

Dunes Spring Up

Dunes form around things that get in the way of wind-blown sand, such as rocks, shrubs, and fence posts. Sand piles up first in drifts and then in dunes. Even an object as tiny as an anthill can form the nucleus of a huge dune.

Meanwhile, farmers in poor countries, such as the nations of western Africa, keep clearing the dry grasslands that border deserts. One reason is the region's growing population. More people need more food. Another reason is the damage caused by irrigation. Farmers must find new land when their old farmland is ruined by salts left behind when irrigation water dries up. When farmers clear these new dry grasslands, they clear away the plants that protect the topsoil from **erosion** by wind and water. Soon, the soil at the surface either washes away or dries up and blows away, leaving more desert behind.

Windblown sand and moving dunes also make more desert. Sand dunes do not sit still. Little by little, the wind moves them along, sometimes as far as 100 feet (30 m) a year. When dunes advance onto neighboring grasslands, the grass dies, and more desert is made. Each year, thousands of square miles of grassland that borders deserts erode and turn into more desert. This damaging process is known as **desertification.** Most desertification takes place in poor nations.

Trying to Help

People are trying new strategies to conserve precious water in deserts. To water their crops, more farmers in desert areas are using trickle-drip irrigation. Holes in networks of plastic pipes deliver directly to plant roots. Old-style sprinkler systems spray water into the air, where it evaporates. The trickle-drip method irrigates more land with less water.

To halt desertification, people living at the edges of deserts cover sand dunes with boulders and fence them in. They also blanket desert sand and soil with grids of straw, then plant shrubs and trees inside the straw squares. Together, the grids and plants keep the sand and soil anchored and stop the desert's advance.

In some parts of the world, people try to stop deserts from spreading. In other places, such as the United States, people try to keep deserts and the life they support from disappearing. Every year, more wild desert land in the United States disappears because of human activities. People clear desert land and cover it with farmland, roads, houses, and cities. All this human activity destroys desert **habitats.** This means that each year, more desert species are in danger of disappearing entirely.

There are people and organizations dedicated to protecting life in the desert. One is the Center for Biological Diversity in Tucson, Arizona. Its executive director has a few suggestions on how to help preserve deserts:

The best thing to do is volunteer at a local environmental group. They all have good projects for young people to plug into. Or start your own conservation club. There are lots of activists, teachers, and biologists who can help your club find simple, meaningful ways to ensure the desert remains wild and beautiful long after your own kids are in school.

Principal Hot Deserts of the World

Name	Facts	Plants and Animals
The Arabian Desert covers most of the Arabian Peninsula, including Saudi Arabia, Iraq, and Israel.	In the south, the *Rub' al-Khali*, or Empty Quarter, is the world's largest uninhabited sand sea.	Acacia tree, slatbush, oleander Locust, camel, gazelle, lizard, jackal, bat
The Australian Desert includes the Great Sandy, Gibson, Simpson, and Great Victoria deserts.	Deserts occupy 80 percent of the Australian continent. The most remote parts are known as the bush, the outback, and the never-never.	Spinifex grass, acacia bush, boab tree Fat-tailed mouse, kangaroo, dingo, platypus, catfish
The Kalahari Desert in southern Africa covers parts of Botswana, Namibia, and South Africa.	The Kalahari Desert is the land of the Bushman peoples, hunter-gatherers who have lived there for at least twenty thousand years.	Dry grass, acacia tree, papyrus Antelope, gerbil, ground squirrel, weaverbird
The Sahara Desert stretches across northern Africa from the Red Sea to the Atlantic Ocean.	Earth's largest desert covering an area nearly as large as the United States: 3.5 million square miles (9 million sq km)	Desert grass, shrubs, trees Snake, lizard, gerbil, fox, sheep
The Sonoran, Mojave, and Chihuahuan deserts cover parts of the American Southwest and northern Mexico.	They contain the U.S. cities of Phoenix, Arizona, and El Paso, Texas. In 1965, astronauts explored the Sonoran Desert craters as training for the first moon landing.	Creosote bush, saguaro cactus, mesquite, Joshua tree, snapdragon Roadrunner, desert pupfish, scorpion, harvester ant, bullfrog
The Thar Desert covers northwestern India and part of Pakistan.	*Thar* means "sandy waste." In May 1974, India exploded its first nuclear device in the Thar.	Grasses, shrubs, acacia bush Desert fox, Indian spiny-tailed lizard, sand grouse, falcon

Principal Cold Deserts of the World

Name	Facts	Plants and Animals
The Atacama Desert runs in a narrow strip averaging 62 miles (100 km) wide along the western coast of Chile.	The landscape of this desert, the driest on Earth, has been compared to the surface of the Moon.	Cactus, bunchgrass Scorpion, lizard, seabird, finch
The Central Asian Deserts occupy parts of the Asian republics of the former Soviet Union, the Himalaya Mountains of Tibet and Nepal, and southeastern Mongolia and northern China.	One of these deserts, the Gobi, is the source of some of the greatest fossil finds in history, including the first dinosaur eggs ever found.	Acacia, salt-resistant shrubs, succulent grass, rhododendron, mountain grass Darkling beetle, termite, badger, lynx, mouse, lark, warbler, yak, sheep, pheasant, snow leopard
The Great Basin Desert, a series of rain-shadow deserts, covers parts of Oregon, Idaho, Wyoming, Colorado, Utah, and Nevada.	The Great Basin Desert is the biggest and coldest desert in the United States. Elevations range from 3,000 to 6,500 feet (915 to 1,981 m).	Sagebrush, saltbrush, greasewood Grasshopper, toad, lizard, snake, sage grouse, jackrabbit, antelope, bighorn sheep
The Namib Desert runs in a narrow strip along the Atlantic coast of Namibia and South Africa.	The Sossusvlei sand dunes are 985 feet (300 m) high, the highest in the world. The edge of the Namib is known as the Skeleton Coast, where sunken ships are said to house the bones of many shipwreck victims.	Desert flower (in Namaqualand area of South Africa) Darkling beetle, fringe-toed lizard, sidewinder, gecko, ostrich, antelope, cuckoo, eagle
The Polar Deserts are in the Arctic region, including Greenland, and in the interior of Antarctica.	Antarctica is the highest of all continents. Average elevation of the rock surface is 8,000 feet (2,440 m) above sea level.	Lichen, moss, pearlwort, meadow grass, arctic white heather Wolf, polar bear, caribou, crane, musk ox, penguin, seal, mite, lice, flea

Glossary

aquifer—an underground area of porous rocks that store water

biome—a region with its own life forms and climate, such as a rain forest or desert

carnivore—a meat-eating animal

coastal desert—a desert that lies alongside an ocean

desert—a dry region that receives less than 10 inches (25 cm) of rain per year

desertification—the process by which more desert land is created over time

dormant—a state of semi-sleep in which organisms temporarily withdraw from the outside environment

dune—a mound or ridge of loose sand heaped by the wind

erosion—the wearing away of something, such as soil

evaporate—when moisture in the air changes from liquid to gas

fossil water—water accumulated from rain and melted snow that fell thousands of years ago

habitat—the natural place where plants and animals grow and live

herbivore—a plant-eating animal

high-altitude desert—a desert located on a high plateau or mountain range

nomads—desert people who move from place to place with their herds or flocks of animals

oasis (plural oases)—a rare pocket of moist, green land in a desert

photosynthesis—the process by which green plants manufacture their own food using carbon dioxide, sunlight, chlorophyll, and water

polar desert—a desert in the Arctic or Antarctic region

rain forest—a forest of tall trees in a region where the climate is warm year round

rain shadow desert—a desert that lies on or near the leeward side of a mountain range

stomata—tiny pores in leaves used in transpiration

symbiotic relationship—when different organisms cooperate to keep one another alive and well

taproot—a long plant root that grows straight down

transpiration—the process plants use to release water vapor and oxygen and take in carbon dioxide through their stomata for photosynthesis

To Find Out More

Books

Allaby, Michael. *Deserts*. New York: Facts On File, Inc., 2000.

Le Rochais, Marie-Ange. *Desert Trek*. New York: Walker & Company, 2001.

MacMahon, James A. *Deserts: The Audubon Society Nature Guides*. New York: Alfred A. Knopf, 1985.

MacQuitty, Miranda. *Desert*. New York: Dorling Kindersley, 2000.

Rumford, James. *Traveling Man: The Journey of Ibn Battuta, 1325–1354*. Boston: Houghton Mifflin Company, 2001.

Videos and DVDs

Eyewitness—Desert, DK Publishing, 1996.

National Geographic's Namib Desert—Africa's Hostile Dunes, Questar Video, 1998.

Organizations and Online Sites

The Arizona-Sonora Desert Museum
2021 North Kinney Road
Tucson, AZ 85743
(520) 883-2702
www.desertmuseum.org
This site contains lots of information on the Sonoran Desert and research projects that the museum staff is conducting.

Center for Biological Diversity
PO Box 710
Tucson, AZ 85702-0710
(520) 623-5252
www.biologicaldiversity.org/swcbd/index.html
This national organization is dedicated to protecting endangered species and wild places. The Species section of the site has detailed information on endangered desert animals and plants.

DesertUSA

www.desertusa.com

This site contains a wide variety of information about U.S. deserts, including facts about plants and animals, maps, and lots of pictures. It also lists current temperatures at different desert sites.

Enchanted Learning

PO Box 321

Mercer Island, WA 98040-0321

www.zoomdinosaurs.com/biomes/desert/desert.shtml

This site contains detailed information on desert animals from around the world.

World Wildlife Fund

1250 Twenty-Fourth Street, NW

PO Box 97180

Washington, DC 20090-7180

(800) CALL-WWF

http://www.worldwildlife.org

The Kids section of this site has games, puzzles, and wildlife information.

A Note on Sources

I began work on this book by jotting down everything I could remember about the time I have spent in the world's deserts. Then I went to my local library and read all the best books and magazine articles I could find on deserts and desert life.

By then, I had several thousand words of notes. I typed out these notes on my laptop computer and organized them into categories, which eventually became the book's chapters and subheadings.

I also e-mailed people at ecology and desert Web sites. I asked educators and directors of conservation organizations questions, and their answers helped direct my research. In particular, I want to thank Kieran Suckling, executive director of the Center for Biological Diversity. I also want to thank Melissa Palestro for giving me the opportunity to write this book and for contributing the editorial rain that helped bring it to life.

—*Ron Fridell*

Index

Numbers in *italics* indicate illustrations.

About the Author

Ron Fridell has traveled to deserts in India, Iran, Israel, Mexico, and the American Southwest. He has floated in the Dead Sea, taken bumpy rides on camels, and slept on sand dunes beneath glittering stars. He is the author of other Watts Library science books, including *Global Warming, Amphibians in Danger: A Worldwide Warning,* and *The Search for Poison Dart Frogs.* He travels to libraries to speak about his books and to middle schools and high schools to give workshops on nonfiction writing.